DEAL BREAKERS

Michele Avantario
and
Maia Dunkel

Broadway Books ❧ New York

DEAL BREAKERS

When Does Mr. Right Become Mr. Not-on-Your-Life?

BROADWAY

Broadway Books titles may be purchased for business or promotional use or for special sales. For information, please write to: Special Markets Department, Random House, Inc., 1745 Broadway, New York, NY 10019.

PRINTED IN THE UNITED STATES OF AMERICA

BROADWAY BOOKS and its logo, a letter B bisected on the diagonal, are trademarks of Random House, Inc.

Visit our Web site at www.broadwaybooks.com

First edition published 2005

Book design by Caroline Cunningham

Library of Congress Cataloging-in-Publication Data
Avantario, Michele.
    Deal Breakers : when does Mr. Right become Mr. Not-on-your-life / Michele Avantario & Maia Dunkel.
        p. cm.
        1. Man-woman relationships. 2. Dating (Social customs) I. Dunkel, Maia.
    II. Title.

HQ801.A838 2005
306.7—dc22

                                                        2004058592

ISBN 0-7679-1933-5

10 9 8 7 6 5 4 3 2 1

To my mother, Margaret,
for teaching me to never settle for anything less than
everything I want. —M.A.

For my sister, Katia,
whom I admire and adore. —M.D.

AND

To all the men we loved before.
And all the others we dated in between.
Thanks for the material.

Contents

DEAL BREAKERS

Introduction

*P*icture it: You've been on a fabulous first date with a guy and are looking forward to seeing him again. He calls to ask you out again and offers to pick you up. When he pulls up in his car, you notice the floor is littered with fast-food wrappers, empty soda cans, and dog hair, and it smells like something died in there. Do you suddenly feel the urge to go back in the house and curl up with a good book, or do you hold your breath and jump in, hoping date number three is down the road?

What are the things you won't tolerate after date number one? What would send you packing after year three? Are you out of there because he waxes his eyebrows even though he's vice president of a bank? We all have things on which we are not willing to compromise. When do you decide to cash in the relationship chips? Whether it's your first date or a long-term relationship, you've got to know your deal breakers!

A deal breaker is something that causes you to change your mind about the person or the relationship. It's that thing about someone which makes you say, "You're not the one for me." Everyone has them. They are personal and can be anything from a pet peeve to a moral issue. A deal breaker lets us know when Mr. Perfect suddenly becomes Mr. Not-a-Chance. Whether you're on a blind date or heading to the altar, it's important to know what you can and won't tolerate in a partner.

Think about your past relationships. Were there flags raised during the first month, the first date, heck, even the first phone call . . . signs indicating things weren't going to work out, but you didn't recognize them? Do you even know what the signs were? How about when the only contact number he'll give is his pager or when he says he's only available to see you on weeknights? What about when the first date's over and you realize he talked nonstop about himself but didn't ask one question about you? How big do the flags need to be as they're waving at you?

We've all been there: in a relationship long after it was dead and buried. Forget about trying to "land a man in twenty days or less" or persuading him to pop the question. First you've got to get rid of the wrong guy so you even have a *chance* at meeting the right one.

While we were traveling for work, we met men and women from all over the world. When you're working on a television shoot for ten hours a day, you cover a lot of ground in conversations, and we found that talking about deal breakers was the ultimate icebreaker. No matter where they were from or whether they were single or married, every person we spoke with had an opinion about what their deal breakers were. It was the one topic that got everyone together debating for hours. We were continually amazed at how different people are in terms of what they are willing to tolerate; what would send one of us heading for the hills, another of us wouldn't bat our eyelashes over.

Ninety-nine percent of the scenarios in this book are true. While some of them are just plain funny and others more thought-provoking, we guarantee they will spark lively, heated discussion. Want to know if you find the quirks of others charming or inexcusable? *Deal Breakers* exposes *real* relationship issues and challenges you to decide how to deal with them.

There are no rules in *Deal Breakers*. This book should be used as a tool to explore your inner thoughts and feelings on relationships and the issues that surround them. *Deal Breakers* will help empower you to determine what you really want in a partner and open your eyes to what you truly want out of life. Why should you settle for a guy who doesn't want children when you've always dreamed of being a mother? Why stay with a guy who refuses to see foreign films when that's your favorite way of spending a Friday night? *Deal Breakers* is not about not compromising in a relationship; it's about not compromising on who to be in a relationship with.

Bring *Deal Breakers* along as entertainment for girls' night out, for a good laugh over dinner with friends, as a stress-buster during a group vacation, or use it as a game during a bachelorette party. Find out who's quick to cut their losses and who's long-suffering. There are no right or wrong answers—only answers that are right or wrong for you.

Deal Breakers will help you identify Mr. Wrong so you can clear the pathway for *your* Mr. Right!

"And Your Half Comes To . . ."

The First Date

*Y*ou agree to pick up your date, since you've got the wheels. You're singing along to your favorite song when he abruptly changes the radio station without asking. *Deal breaker?*

*O*n your first date you notice he's had four glasses of wine to your one before the entrée even arrives. *Deal breaker?*

*Y*ou're walking to the restaurant with your date. When you arrive, he proceeds to open the door for himself and walk right in front of you. *Deal breaker?*

*Y*ou're anxiously waiting for your blind date to arrive. When you open the door to let him in, you see he's sporting a diamond earring bigger and flashier than you could ever imagine having on your ring finger. *Deal breaker?*

You're at a first-date brunch with a really cute guy and enjoying his tales about traveling around the world. When you get home you realize he didn't ask one question about you. *Deal breaker?*

You're at a lovely restaurant with the guy you'd been hoping would ask you out for a while. Just as you are about to take your first bite, he grabs his fork and helps himself to your meal without asking. *Deal breaker?*

You've just enjoyed a nice dinner with a guy and hope a second date is in the cards. He walks you to your door and just as he leans in to give you a kiss, his very bad breath makes you want to run for the hills. *Deal breaker?*

It's been months since your last date and you're excited about a night out on the town. Your date picks you up at eight and drives to the nearest pizza parlor for a slice. *Deal breaker?*

You're out together for the first time in a chic restaurant when your date tells you he can't turn off his cell phone because he's waiting for an important call. When the call comes in you learn it was to get basketball scores. *Deal breaker?*

♛

You're having a pleasant time with your blind date dining in a nice restaurant. The bill arrives and your date pays, but you notice he doesn't leave a tip. When you point out his error, he explains he only leaves a tip when the service is exceptional. *Deal breaker?*

🐸

You're excited to get this first dinner date under way, but before the appetizer arrives, he asks you how many people you've slept with. *Deal breaker?*

*Y*our blind date gets a reservation at the best Italian restaurant in town and you're having a hard time deciding between the snapper and the veal. The waiter approaches and just as you're about to speak, your date jumps in and orders for you. *Deal breaker?*

*Y*ou're on your first date with a guy, having dinner at your favorite restaurant. As far as you're concerned, date number two is definitely going to happen. When the bill arrives, he reaches across the table to pick it up. He looks at it and then passes it over to you so you can figure out how much your half comes to. *Deal breaker?*

*Y*ou're on a plane heading out for a weeklong business trip the day after a first date. You arrive at your hotel to find a very expensive bouquet of flowers with a card that reads, "Thanks so much for last night. Miss you already. I'll be thinking about you!" *Deal breaker?*

*Y*our blind date snaps at the waiter when he brings out the wrong entrée. At the end of the meal he demands that the waiter remove the price of his entrée from the bill to compensate for the hassle. *Deal breaker?*

♛

*Y*our first date with a guy is coming to a close and he offers to drive you home. As you approach his car, you notice his bumper sticker reads, "It's God's job to take care of Osama bin Laden. It's up to *us* to arrange the meeting." *Deal breaker?*

🐸

*Y*our date arrives twenty minutes late and apologizes profusely. He goes on to explain that he has issues with time and you should know up front he's *always* late. *Deal breaker?*

*Y*our date springs for a horse-and-carriage ride in the park. During the ride the horse stops to relieve itself and your guy doubles over in laughter at the horse's "monstrous dump" and goes on to tell you that it rivals his own "record-holding load." *Deal breaker?*

♛

*Y*our blind date picks you up for dinner and a movie. While getting into the car you notice a police department parking pass on the dashboard. When you say, "Funny, I thought you worked in engineering," he says he does and explains he got the pass through a friend. *Deal breaker?*

*Y*ou're on your first date with a guy who orders soup for an appetizer. Just as he's finishing his last spoonful, he picks up the bowl and starts slurping away. *Deal breaker?*

onversation is flowing with your date and he asks to know your astrological sign. When you tell him Virgo, he says in complete seriousness that your relationship will probably not go anywhere because he's a Sagittarius. *Deal breaker?*

You've agreed to go out on a blind date with a guy at your best friend's request. Three hours into the date, he says, "I can't believe how well this is going. After our initial phone call, I thought for sure I'd be outta here after the first drink." *Deal breaker?*

wo days after the first date you come home to a message on your machine from him wondering where you are because he's sure you didn't have any plans tonight. He's also left a message on your cell phone asking where you are and that you call him immediately so he knows you're safe. *Deal breaker?*

*Y*ou've enjoyed a nice first date and he offers to drive you home. In the car he slips in a CD of *La Traviata* and starts singing along to the arias out of tune. *Deal breaker?*

*T*he cute guy you've been eyeing asks you out on a date. When you excuse yourself to go to the ladies' room, he gives you a wink and says, "I hope everything comes out OK!" *Deal breaker?*

*Y*ou're on a first date and during the conversation you learn he's never dated anyone longer than three months. *Deal breaker?*

*Y*ou're on your first date and before you order, you know more about his ex-girlfriend than you do about him. *Deal breaker?*

Your best friend took the liberty of setting you up. During the date you notice the conversation keeps turning back to his high school years, which he describes as the "time of his life"; he wishes he could "do it all over again." *Deal breaker?*

You've been set up on a blind date with a divorcé. You're enjoying the conversation. When you ask how long he's been divorced, he replies, "From that bitch? About five years." *Deal breaker?*

You've been set up on a blind date and agree to meet at a bar for some billiards and beer. When he walks in the door, you can't help but notice he's sporting a fanny pack. *Deal breaker?*

Spring has sprung and you're off to a blind date at a steak house. When you ask how you'll recognize him, he says he'll be "the one in shorts," When you remind him it's still chilly, he explains he has a rule by which he doesn't wear long pants after April 1. *Deal breaker?*

Meeting Mr. Johnson

Sex

*Y*ou've been seeing a guy and upon entering his apartment for the first time, you notice a book on his coffee table called *The Idiot's Guide to Sex*. *Deal breaker?*

*Y*ou're on a date and ask to know the most embarrassing thing he's ever done. He tells you that one night in college he got so drunk, he made out with his fraternity brother. *Deal breaker?*

*T*he night has finally come to consummate your relationship. Just as he's about to go down on you, he suggests you go out and get a full waxing next time because he "only visits Bush Gardens once." *Deal breaker?*

*Y*ou're dating a guy who wants to try a ménage-à-trois for his birthday. *Deal breaker?*

*Y*ou're feeling a little frisky and agree to go up to your date's apartment for a little *"je ne sais quoi."* While getting down and dirty, he opens a drawer, whips out a vibrator, and asks if his "battery-operated friend" can join the party. *Deal breaker?*

*Y*ou're engaging in a smooch session with your new guy at his place. He makes it quite clear that he's up for sex, but you tell him you're not ready. He gets huffy and asks for a hand job, since it's the "least you can do." *Deal breaker?*

*Y*ou're getting married in six months and attending a premarital counseling class required by your religion. The counselor advises you not to have sex before the wedding. You'd really like to try to wait until your honeymoon but your fiancé refuses to consider that an option. *Deal breaker?*

*Y*ou're dating a thirty-year-old guy with whom you'd like to get serious. You think tonight's *the* night but he lets you know he's still a virgin "waiting for the right woman." *Deal breaker?*

※

*Y*ou and your guy have a fabulous sex life. One day while at his apartment, you go into his closet to grab a sweatshirt. You notice a suspicious-looking box and your curiosity gets the better of you. You open it to find it's filled with all kinds of porn—books, toys, videos, magazines, you name it. *Deal breaker?*

*Y*ou and your new love interest just spent a great night together. When grabbing some toothpaste from his medicine cabinet, you discover a prescription for Viagra. You ask him about it and he explains he likes to use it for "a little kick-start." *Deal breaker?*

*Y*ou and your guy are getting serious and have decided it's time to sleep together. The night has arrived and when you get to the "Do you have a condom?" part, he says, "Isn't it your job to take care of that stuff?" *Deal breaker?*

*Y*ou've decided that tonight's the night with your new guy and it seems he's on the same page. Things quickly get hot and heavy, and before you know it he shouts, "Who's your Daddy?" *Deal breaker?*

*Y*ou're getting serious with someone who lets you know he contracted herpes from an earlier relationship. It's under control but, of course, there's a good chance you could get it too. *Deal breaker?*

*Y*our boyfriend wants to spice things up and encourages a game of "Sex Fantasies Come True!" He volunteers to go first and makes a beeline for the bathroom. When he emerges he's wearing a diaper and says, "Mommy, I've been a bad boy and I think I deserve a spanking."
Deal breaker?

*A*fter two weeks of heaving petting, you and your guy have decided this weekend is *it*. He books a romantic bed-and-breakfast, and just when you think your two worlds are about to collide, you discover his penis is so small you could probably get more action from a super tampon. *Deal breaker?*

*T*hings are getting serious with the new man and you've noticed that while he's enjoyed many a blow job from you, he hasn't reciprocated the favor. When you ask what gives, he tells you going down is not "part of his repertoire." *Deal breaker?*

You had figured it was a one-time thing, but you've noticed that every time you're in the middle of a very heated moment with your guy, he starts talking baby talk. *Deal breaker?*

After two years of monogamy your partner tells you he wants to go out swinging. But because he knows you're not open to it, he wants you to "fantasy swing," where you pretend to be other women, specifically women you and he socialize with. *Deal breaker?*

Sex with your new guy has been great but the second he's finished, he hops right into the shower. One night when you try to squeeze in a cuddle after making love, he tells you he needs to "get clean" before he can do anything else. *Deal breaker?*

While you're making out with your new flame, he asks you to unbutton his pants so he can formally introduce you to "Mr. Johnson," your new "best friend." *Deal breaker?*

You and your love interest get into a conversation about relationships and he tells you he believes any woman who's had sex with more than three men before marriage is a slut. *Deal breaker?*

You're dating a guy who tells you he's been to a "high class" prostitute in the past. He explains he used to travel extensively for business and didn't have time to date, so that was an "easy and safe option" to satisfy him at the time. *Deal breaker?*

*Y*ou and your new flame have enjoyed the three-month-let's-just-stay-in-tonight honeymoon stage and you're now ready to venture out into the real world. A couple of outings later you notice that every time you introduce your new boyfriend to one of your guy friends, he says, "Yeah right, 'friends.' Newsflash: guys are only friends with women they want to sleep with." *Deal breaker?*

❀

*Y*ou're getting serious with a guy and you think it's the best sex ever. One night while you're rolling in the hay, he suggests you buy a book on the art of blow jobs so you can master the trade. *Deal breaker?*

No Way with PDA

Romance

*T*he dapper businessman you've been flirting with on your flight asks to escort you home. The car pulls up in front of your building and you're hoping he'll lean in for a kiss. Instead he turns to you and says, "So, do you want to do it or what?" *Deal breaker?*

👍

*Y*ou're camping with a group of friends. After melting many a marshmallow by the fire, your new guy wants to retire to your tent for a little "kumbaya." You point out that everyone will be able to hear you and he says, "I know, that's the beauty of it." *Deal breaker?*

👎

*Y*ou've made it to second base with your new guy, but you're not yet ready to go all the way. Several dates later he tells you he's tired of holding at third and won't play the game if he can't hit a home run. *Deal breaker?*

You meet a really attractive guy and can't wait for the first kiss. He finally leans in but instead of fireworks, you feel his tongue darting in and out of your mouth like a snake's. *Deal breaker?*

👍

Midway into your first make-out session you are taken aback when your date licks your armpit and tells you he can't wait to get all your clothes off because he "loves the way you taste." *Deal breaker?*

👎

You've noticed over a period of five months that every time your boyfriend wants to get it on, he pops in a movie like *Pulp Fiction* or *Scarface*. When you ask him about it he says the violence turns him on.
Deal breaker?

*I*n the three months you and your guy have been dating, you've come close to having sex a dozen times, but he always backs off in the heat of the moment. You're hoping tonight's the night, so you break out your sexiest lingerie, light a few candles, and pour some wine. Later you're on the couch fooling around and just when you think it's about to happen, he jumps up and says he's just not ready. *Deal breaker?*

👎

*Y*ou've started dating a guy who's gotten into the habit of making "booty calls" to you in the middle of the night after hours of bar-hopping with the guys. *Deal breaker?*

👍

*Y*ou're loving the fact that your guy is a manly man who dons a five o'clock shadow and looks great in a pair of Levi's. After some time you notice in bed he only talks dirty. When you try to encourage more romantic talk, he suggests you go read a Harlequin romance novel. *Deal breaker?*

You've gone out on several dates with a guy you're really excited about. One morning upon entering your office, you discover a box of chocolates on your desk with a handwritten note that reads: "Dear Alison, Thanks so much for a fantastic three dates! I'll call you soon. Best, Mike." What could be better? Too bad your name is Kara. *Deal breaker?*

☞

The chemistry between you and your guy is electric, but you've noticed he can't go an hour without smacking your ass or grabbing your breast, especially in public. *Deal breaker?*

👍

Your fiancé offers to pay for a boob job for your birthday because he believes you'll look and feel better with a bigger rack. *Deal breaker?*

*Y*ou and your man decide to take a beach vacation together and he offers to plan it. When you arrive at your bungalow and put on your bathing suit, he tells you there's no need because it's a nude beach.
Deal breaker?

👍

*Y*ou're looking forward to a romantic Valentine's evening with your new guy. He picks you up at seven and when you get in the car he says, "So what's the plan?" *Deal breaker?*

👎

*Y*our birthday has arrived and the guy you're dating shows up with a beautifully wrapped gift. You open it up to find a very lacy, and what looks to be a quite revealing, shirt. He begs you to try it on and says, "I was thinking this could be your Anna Nicole look!"
Deal breaker?

*Y*our date invites you to go for a walk in the park since the weather is so spectacular. When you motion to hold his hand, he pushes it away claiming he's "not a believer in PDA." *Deal breaker?*

👍

*Y*ou've been dating a guy for a year and Valentine's Day is this Saturday. He calls to ask if he could give you flowers on Monday since it's cheaper and more practical as you're both going out of town for the weekend. *Deal breaker?*

👎

*Y*ou've just started dating a guy you really like and one day you come home to find him sporting your favorite Betsy Johnson dress. He tells you wearing women's clothes turns him on and motions for you to put on his tux, which is laid out on the bed. *Deal breaker?*

Licking the Last Stamp

Commitment

You've hit the five-month mark with your man and are really into the relationship. One night you're over at a friend's house and she tells you she recently signed up for Internet dating. While scanning the photos with her for potentials, you come across a recently posted profile of your boyfriend. *Deal breaker?*

♥

Your man of a few months kisses another girl at a party and you happen to see it. The next day while discussing it, he blames his actions on the alcohol. *Deal breaker?*

♥

You're pretty sure your boyfriend is gearing up to propose. One night you overhear a conversation between him and one of his friends in which you learn he's having second thoughts. *Deal breaker?*

*Y*ou're looking to settle down. You meet a great guy who's five years your junior. About two months after dating, he lets you know he loves being single and is nowhere near ready to be in a committed relationship. *Deal breaker?*

*Y*ou fantasize about marrying the guy you're seeing. One evening during a tête-à-tête, he lets you know he cares about you and wants to continue with the relationship, but doesn't believe you're "the one." *Deal breaker?*

*T*hings are going well with the guy you've been dating. When you tell him you're so happy to have found a "best friend" in him, he tells you he considers you a great lover, but *not* his best friend. *Deal breaker?*

*Y*ou and your fiancé are eight months away from your wedding date. One night he tells you he had a meaningless one-night stand on a business trip when you were first dating. He says he wants to come clean so there are no secrets between you before you make the ultimate commitment. *Deal breaker?*

♥

*A*fter more than two years of your guy talking nonstop about getting married, the invitations are finally going out. Just as you're licking the last stamp, he tells you he's having second thoughts and wants to postpone the wedding because he's "nervous and not feeling quite ready." *Deal breaker?*

💔

*Y*ou and your man of three years are spending a quiet evening at home watching *Casablanca*. During the closing credits you turn to him and re-profess your love. He then turns to you and says he loves you too, but he's not sure he's still *in love* with you. *Deal breaker?*

You are dating a guy six years your junior. After an exciting and romantic year together, he hasn't said, "I love you." You've said it to him numerous times, but he hesitates, explaining he's scared because he's "never said it before." *Deal breaker?*

♥

You and your boyfriend have been through your ups and downs, but you believe the time has come to settle down. One evening while making dinner, you initiate a discussion about the future. He lets you know he won't even entertain the idea of marriage yet because he wants "at least three more years of freedom" before his "life sentence." *Deal breaker?*

💔

You've been dating a guy for a couple of months and one night when you ask where the relationship is going, he says, "Who knows? But you're a cool girl and we're just having some fun, right?" *Deal breaker?*

*Y*ou and your new guy have recently had the "let's-be-exclusive-since-we've-already-slept-together" conversation. One Friday night while at his apartment, the machine picks up when he's in the shower. It's another woman confirming their date for tomorrow night and thanking him for Tuesday. *Deal breaker?*

💔

*Y*ou and your guy have been dating for two years and you're frustrated with the fact that he never seems to remember your birthday or anniversary. When you drop hints that an important date is coming around the bend, he says, "Why don't you just grab my wallet and pick out something nice for yourself?" *Deal breaker?*

♥

*Y*ou've hit the three-month mark and your boyfriend comes over to celebrate. He hands you a greeting card, but oddly there's no personal message or signature. *Deal breaker?*

*Y*our guy gets on one knee and you're about ready to faint. He begins the proposal noting how many great years you've spent together, and closes with: "So we might as well do it now before we change our minds, right?" *Deal breaker?*

♥

*Y*ou're so happy because you know you've found Mr. Right. One night when discussing the future, he lets you know he's committed to you for life but doesn't believe in the institution of marriage. *Deal breaker?*

♥

*Y*ou find out your fiancé is having a stripper at his bachelor party. You're uncomfortable but know it's "tradition" so you go along with it. The next day he openly admits the stripper performed oral sex on him. *Deal breaker?*

BYOP (Bring Your Own Popcorn)

Money

*Y*ou're dating a guy who urges you to loan him a large sum of money for his independent film project. He promises to have the money back to you in six months. *Deal breaker?*

*Y*ou're engaged to the man of your dreams—and he's wealthy too! A couple of months before the wedding, he tells you he expects you to sign a prenuptial agreement. *Deal breaker?*

*Y*our new guy is a struggling actor. Because he's not getting enough work he decides to move back in with his parents until finances turn around. He says he doesn't want to take any other job because it would take away from his primary focus. *Deal breaker?*

*Y*ou're dating a man who holds a respectable job and lives in a bare studio apartment. After a couple of months, you learn he won $250,000 in the lottery two years ago, but blew it all on an expensive Italian sports car. *Deal breaker?*

*Y*ou're engaged, and just before the wedding your fiancé tells you out of the blue that he has left his high-paying job as a business consultant to try his hand at painting. *Deal breaker?*

*Y*ou meet a cute guy at a bar and he invites you to dinner the next night. Just as he's about to sign the bill, the waiter comes back with a pair of scissors to let your date know his credit card was denied and it must be destroyed. *Deal breaker?*

*Y*ou're engaged to the man of your dreams. One day while out shopping you see his bounced check taped up on the grocery store wall. When you confront him about it, he brushes it off as a one-time mistake. *Deal breaker?*

*Y*ou and your guy are planning a two-week trip together to the Florida Keys. You suggest a couple of hotels that were recommended to you, but he explains he never stays at hotels and prefers to crash at friends' houses. *Deal breaker?*

*Y*our date suggests a great Mexican place for dinner. The margaritas and conversation are flowing. When the bill arrives, he fishes out some cash and a coupon and asks the waitress if it's still valid. *Deal breaker?*

*Y*our date invites you to a movie and kindly lets you choose the film. When you ask if he wouldn't mind getting some popcorn, he says he already took care of it and shows you the bag of snacks he brought from home. He goes on to say that anyone who pays the outrageous prices at the theater is getting ripped off. *Deal breaker?*

*A*t the end of dinner your date asks to borrow twenty dollars because he's short some cash. He says he'll pay you back the next time you see each other, but three dates go by and there's no mention of the twenty bucks. *Deal breaker?*

*T*he past couple of times you've been out to drinks with your new beau, he jokes that you should pick up the tab more often since you make more money. *Deal breaker?*

*Y*ou and your date are heading out to the parking lot after seeing a movie when you discover his car is being towed. Later you find out he owes $800 in unpaid tickets. *Deal breaker?*

*Y*ou're dating a guy who tells you he broke up with his last girlfriend because she wasn't driven enough. When you ask her profession, he says she's a teacher and therefore has no chance of making any real money. *Deal breaker?*

*Y*ou've finally met the guy of your dreams. He may have come from the "wrong side of the tracks" but he's college educated, works in an investment bank, and loves the great outdoors just like you. One day you ask how he was able to pay for college and he tells you openly and honestly he worked as a stripper (and occasional escort) in a local club for four years. *Deal breaker?*

Mommy Dearest

Family

You're just about to spend your first night at his place when you notice he keeps an 8" x 10" picture of his mother on his bedside table. *Deal breaker?*

♛

You've been dating a guy for about a year and feel that things are getting serious. He's met your friends and family but you haven't met anyone on his side. You know his sister's wedding is approaching and figure that will be the perfect time to meet everyone. Another week goes by, he hasn't mentioned anything about the wedding, and when you bring it up, he says he'll only be gone for four days. *Deal breaker?*

You find out your boyfriend of six months has been bad-mouthing your sister to his friends. *Deal breaker?*

*T*he guy you've been flirting with from your apartment building finally asks you out. After several dates you learn his mother also lives in the building and he goes over to her house every night during the week for dinner. *Deal breaker?*

*A*fter a few weeks of dating someone, you learn he stays in constant contact with his ex. He has Caller ID, and you notice that every time she calls and you pick up the phone, she hangs up. *Deal breaker?*

*Y*ou're living with a guy who tells you he promised his parents they can move in upon retirement.
Deal breaker?

*Y*ou've been exclusive with your boyfriend for about a year and one night he proposes. You can't wait to let everyone know, but before you pick up the phone, your fiancé warns you that his parents don't like you because you're "not good enough" for him. *Deal breaker?*

*Y*ou're getting serious with a guy and find out his father is in prison (and will be for at least the next fifteen years). *Deal breaker?*

♛

*Y*ou're engaged to a man who seems to fit perfectly into your family. But then you find out he told his best friend he's dreading having "Mommy Dearest" as his mother-in-law. *Deal breaker?*

🐸

*Y*ou recently started dating a guy you really like. One evening while over at his place, you notice he doesn't have a single family photo displayed. When you ask about his family, he tells you he's severed ties with them but won't discuss with you the reasons why.
Deal breaker?

You're so happy to meet a guy who has a great relationship with his father. It's so good that he religiously spends every Sunday golfing with him at their country club and therefore refuses to make any other plans. *Deal breaker?*

You've been dating a guy for some time and things are going really well. One morning your sister calls to invite you both over for brunch and you accept. When you hang up, your boyfriend suggests it'd be best if you limit seeing each other's families as a couple to once every two months. *Deal breaker?*

You wake up on Sunday morning at your new boyfriend's place to the sound of keys rattling in the door lock. When you emerge from the bedroom to see who it is, he introduces you to his mother, who has stopped by to drop off his laundry and tidy up. *Deal breaker?*

*Y*ou've been dating a man for three months and things are going really well. One weekend your parents invite you both to their cabin. Upon your arrival, your mom shows you to separate rooms. As she heads back downstairs, he says loudly enough for her to hear, "What is this, the 1950s? So much for a fun weekend." *Deal breaker?*

♛

*Y*our new guy is great and you think it's a hoot that he has an identical twin brother. One night, you and your guy are enjoying a romantic dinner for two during which "heavy petting" and "footsy" are the main course. A couple of weeks later, you learn they were playing a trick on you and it was actually the twin who was sitting across from you. Your guy claims it was just "fun and games." *Deal breaker?*

*J*ust before the wedding, your fiancé tells you he doesn't want to have kids, which is not what he told you pre-engagement. *Deal breaker?*

You arrive at the local coffee shop to meet your new guy and see he's on the phone. You can tell he's upset because he's uttered more than one four-letter word. When he hangs up you say, "Serious work problems, huh?" and he says, "No, serious *mother* problems."
Deal breaker?

Previously Engaged

Past Relationships

One night after a few drinks, your date lets you know he once had a passionate long-term affair with a married woman. *Deal breaker?*

You've been dating a guy exclusively for three months. You leave on a business trip for two weeks and, a month later, find out his ex-girlfriend invited him out for a birthday cocktail while you were gone. The only reason you learn about it is because you happen to ask when he saw her last. *Deal breaker?*

Your new love interest, a divorcé of two years, invites you over to dinner at his place. While taking a look around, you notice family pictures adorning every room of the house, all of which include his ex-wife. Eerily, you look a lot like her. *Deal breaker?*

You've been exclusively dating a guy for six months and things are going really well. One Sunday while meeting for brunch with a group of his friends, you find out from the woman seated next to you that he was engaged before—which he has neglected to mention to you. *Deal breaker?*

You've been dating someone for a couple of months, and one night he tells you he called off his previous engagement because he'd been cheating and the guilt was killing him. *Deal breaker?*

You've been on several dates with a guy and find out he owns a restaurant with his ex-wife, which means they have to spend plenty of long nights and weekends in each other's company. *Deal breaker?*

You and a guy from your winter volleyball league are becoming more than great friends. The chemistry is electric but you know it can never be since he's engaged to be married. Later that season he professes his love to you and says he'll break his engagement if there's a chance you'll be with him. *Deal breaker?*

Your new boyfriend explains why he left his ex at the altar: he had an epiphany as she was walking down the aisle that he didn't really love her. *Deal breaker?*

After three months of dating you suggest to your guy it might be time to throw out the stuffed animal his ex-girlfriend gave him—which is prominently displayed in the bedroom. He refuses and explains, "There are a lot of memories tied up in that little chipmunk."
Deal breaker?

Your boyfriend finally pops the question and presents you with a gorgeous ring, which he says he designed just for you! While you're showing it off, his cousin lets you know that your ring is the same one he used when proposing to his ex. *Deal breaker?*

You've gone out on a few dates with a guy who has the cutest golden retriever ever. One day while over at his house, you notice the dog is nowhere to be found. When you ask as to Buster's whereabouts, he says his ex-girlfriend gets him every other weekend as part of their custody agreement. *Deal breaker?*

You're dating a guy who's about ten years older than you, but you don't mind the age difference because he makes up for it in savoir faire. After some time you learn that his past three girlfriends were all about fifteen years younger then he was. *Deal breaker?*

*A*fter three dates, he asks you over to dinner at his place. While finishing up the cooking, he invites you to peruse a photo album sitting on the coffee table. You open it to see it's filled with pictures of him with his exes in various states of undress. *Deal breaker?*

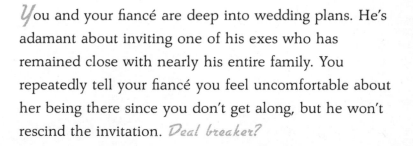

*Y*ou're dating a new guy who constantly brings up his exes and says things like "You're so much prettier than Paula"; "You dress way nicer than Carla"; and "You're so much better in bed than Maria." *Deal breaker?*

*Y*ou and your fiancé are deep into wedding plans. He's adamant about inviting one of his exes who has remained close with nearly his entire family. You repeatedly tell your fiancé you feel uncomfortable about her being there since you don't get along, but he won't rescind the invitation. *Deal breaker?*

Watercooler Casanova

The Workplace

*Y*ou're dating a guy who lets you know he won't take any social calls at work. When you ask about it, he explains he doesn't like to be bothered during business hours. *Deal breaker?*

👍

*Y*ou're dating a guy from work and find out you're both up for a promotion as you're equally qualified. Unfortunately, only one position is open. Two weeks later he gets the job and now he's your boss. *Deal breaker?*

👎

*Y*ou've been dating a guy who you really like for a couple of months. One evening he tells you a story in which a friend from work was asked to leave the company due to alleged sexual harassment. The charges were dropped and your date is adamant about the fact that it was all a lie and the woman was just a "bitch out to get him." *Deal breaker?*

*Y*ou've been dating a guy for a couple of months and one night during dinner, he mentions he was fired from his last four jobs. *Deal breaker?*

👍

*Y*ou're living with your boyfriend, who recently got laid off from his job. Six months have passed, he hasn't found any work, and seems to have lost his motivation to do so. *Deal breaker?*

👎

*Y*our boyfriend has been traveling a lot lately with a new female coworker. One night when you call his hotel room, you hear her giggling in the background. When you ask him about it, he says they're just sharing a bottle of wine and talking office politics. *Deal breaker?*

👍

*Y*ou're dating a guy who, when describing a typical day at his executive job, tells you he kicks back with his feet up on the desk and surfs the Internet most of the day. *Deal breaker?*

*Y*ou're dating a guy who's an undercover agent and therefore can never discuss his job or daily whereabouts. *Deal breaker?*

👎

*Y*ou're involved with a guy who has a high-stress job. One night at a bar you overhear someone telling a story in which he is the main character. Your guy is depicted as a "condescending jerk" who's "totally out of control." When you confront him about it he explains that "work is no place for friendship" and "a true leader has to command respect through fear." *Deal breaker?*

👍

*Y*ou're engaged to a man who lets you know that when you have children he would like to stay home and be a house-husband just like Mr. Mom, meaning it's up to you to bring home the bacon. *Deal breaker?*

*T*he guy you're dating from work (not that you've told anyone) calls you in a panic for help on a big project. It's crunch time and money is at stake. You pull an all-nighter with him, and he goes on to win a bonus of $1,000. He doesn't offer you a cut, and when you congratulate him he says, "Thanks, I really thrive on a high-pressure challenge." *Deal breaker?*

👍

*Y*ou've been flirting with a guy at your company and gone on a couple of dates. Then you hear from a coworker that he's known as a bit of a watercooler Casanova, and has been involved with quite a few women in the company. *Deal breaker?*

👎

*Y*ou and your doctor boyfriend of three months are taking a road trip together. Just two days before you leave, he discovers his car needs to be re-registered. He asks you to do it since he doesn't have time to wait in lines. *Deal breaker?*

*Y*ou invite your boyfriend of three months to a work function and notice that he's hitting it off with everyone quite well. The next day one of your female coworkers approaches to let you know he told everyone you slept together on the first date. *Deal breaker?*

👎

*T*he successful businessman you've been dating just accepted a job that will take him to another country for six months of every year. *Deal breaker?*

👍

*T*hings seem to be going well with the new artist you're dating and he invites you to spend the night. The next morning as you're getting dressed to head out to your corporate job, he asks, "So how do you live with yourself working for 'The Man' every day?" *Deal breaker?*

You've been out on two dates with a guy you met on Match.com and you're excited to be seeing someone who works in the movie business. When you Google his company you discover they specialize in hardcore porn. *Deal breaker?*

👎

You meet a man who's a struggling artist. During the few dates you've had, he talks about his work passionately and is very serious about making painting his career. One day he invites you to his loft for a viewing and you see that his paintings are unmistakably bad. It's not a question of taste. They just suck. *Deal breaker?*

👍

You invite your new boyfriend to a work party, and after a couple of drinks he turns to your boss and says, "She's a pretty good employee, huh?" When your boss agrees, he continues with, "So why are you paying her so little?" *Deal breaker?*

Pickin' and Flickin'

Grooming

*Y*ou're getting serious with a guy and just spent your first romantic night together at your place. The next morning as you're making *café pour deux*, he saunters out of the bathroom using your toothbrush.
Deal breaker?

♥

*Y*ou're on your third date with a guy and discover when he takes off his shirt that his upper arm is branded with a bright-red heart tattoo that reads, "Mike and Antoinette Marianna Forever." *Deal breaker?*

♥

*Y*ou compliment your date on his comfortable-looking flannel pajamas and he says, "Thanks, you can get some great stuff on eBay. That's where I get all my clothes."
Deal breaker?

♥

*Y*ou've just had a session of great sex. Just as you both roll over, you notice he's pickin' and flickin'.
Deal breaker?

$\mathcal{F}$riday night's date was so great that you've already locked in Saturday. Later in the evening when he pulls off his jeans, you notice he's wearing the same Santa Claus boxers he was wearing the night before. *Deal breaker?*

♥

$\mathcal{Y}$ou've just had a nice roll in the hay with your new guy. On your way to the bathroom, you notice his "tighty-whities" are decorated with skid marks. *Deal breaker?*

💔

$\mathcal{Y}$ou're dating a guy who you learn has had a nose job. *Deal breaker?*

♥

$\mathcal{Y}$ou're dating a guy you really like. One night while things are getting hot and heavy, you discover he wears a hairpiece. *Deal breaker?*

*Y*ou and your boyfriend get engaged and decide to marry in exactly one year. Six months pass and he's gone from being athletically trim to a couch potato thirty pounds heavier. It's not a medical problem—he's just let himself go. *Deal breaker?*

♥

*Y*ou can't wait to hop in the sack with your new beau. After a grope here and a feel there, you discover he's wearing some "jewelry" in unusual places. Mid-grope, he asks if his penis piercing is turning you on. *Deal breaker?*

♥

*Y*ou're dating a guy and loving his curly locks. When you tell him facetiously you're a little jealous he says, "Please, you think I was born this way? This look costs me two hundred bucks a pop!" *Deal breaker?*

*Y*ou thought it was just when he met your parents, but you begin to notice that no matter who your guy meets for the first time, he sweats so profusely that he has to excuse himself to "dry off." *Deal breaker?*

♥

*Y*our first couple of dates with the cute lawyer went really well and you're excited about your next date, at the beach. When you arrive, he takes off his shirt and you notice his back hair is so thick you could braid it. *Deal breaker?*

♥

*T*he weather is warming up and you and your date decide to go Rollerblading. He takes off his sweatshirt and you notice he's wearing a thick gold chain that he says he never takes off. *Deal breaker?*

You've been on several casual dates with your new guy and things are going well. After about a month you invite him to a family birthday dinner at a fancy restaurant and he shows up wearing jeans and his favorite concert T-shirt. *Deal breaker?*

♥

Your boyfriend proposes after six months, and before he gets to the words "marry me" you've already said, "Yes!" As a celebration, he comes home with your name tattooed on his arm. *Deal breaker?*

💔

You've been dating a guy you think is perfect for you. He's well dressed, funny, and has a great job. One night he invites you up to his pad, where you discover he has no problem passing gas in front of you. *Deal breaker?*

♥

You're sleeping over at your boyfriend's place for the first time. Just as things get heated, he grabs a towel from the closet and puts it down so you don't "dirty the sheets." *Deal breaker?*

*Y*our boyfriend of two months has been complaining of a toothache for days. When you suggest he go to the dentist to relieve the pain, he mentions he hasn't been since high school. *Deal breaker?*

*Y*ou run into the new guy you're dating at the gym and do a double take when you see he's wearing super-tight white bicycle shorts and a form-fitting tank top. *Deal breaker?*

*Y*ou've been dating for three months when Valentine's Day rolls around. As a surprise, your guy takes you to his favorite spa to treat you to a couple's mani-pedi session. *Deal breaker?*

*Y*ou and your new guy go out on a double date with your brother and his girlfriend to a rib joint. The next day you find out from your brother that your guy didn't wash his hands when leaving the bathroom in between the appetizer and main course. *Deal breaker?*

*Y*ou're dating a guy who tells you about his "going out" ritual, which consists of taking a soothing bath with candles and meditating. He explains it helps him get in the mood, a requirement for him to have a successful date. *Deal breaker?*

♥

*Y*ou and the new guy are getting quite serious. After a couple of months he invites you to dinner at his parents' place. While he's showing you around the house, you notice your very slim and fit boyfriend is extremely overweight in every picture. You later find out he's had gastric-bypass surgery. *Deal breaker?*

💔

*Y*ou're on your third date with a guy, taking a walk around town, and you can't help but notice he incessantly grabs his crotch. *Deal breaker?*

♥

*Y*ou've just enjoyed a second-date dinner. Your date walks you home, and just as he drops you off, you overhear him hocking a loogie. *Deal breaker?*

You're on the phone with your girlfriend when your new guy overhears you complaining about your overly dry and flaky skin. When you hang up, he suggests you try a new exfoliating cream he read about in *Glamour*. He goes on to tell you *Glamour* offers the best skin-care tips. *Deal breaker?*

Potpourri or Pigsty?

Lifestyle

*A*fter a couple of dates with a guy, he invites you up to his apartment for an after-dinner drink. Upon entering, you discover he has three small dogs and he lets you know they all sleep in his bed every night. *Deal breaker?*

*Y*ou call the cat lover you're dating and get his answering machine for the first time. While waiting for the beep you hear the message, "Whiskers, Snuggles, and I aren't home right now but we'll get back to you as soon as we can." *Deal breaker?*

*Y*ou've been dating a guy for a month and he asks you back to his place. When you get there you see he's got quite a few religious items adorning his home. *Deal breaker?*

You're walking down the street with your blind date when he stops at the store to make a quick purchase. While he's filling out the check, you notice it's designed with Disney characters. *Deal breaker?*

You're dating a guy who invites you up to his apartment. You go straight to the living room, which you see is decorated with large Britney Spears and Christina Aguilera posters, or, as he calls them, "art." *Deal breaker?*

You're engaged to a man who lets you know he will never live in the suburbs. You, meanwhile, have been dreaming of living in a house with an expansive backyard and a white picket fence. *Deal breaker?*

You're engaged to a man of another religion and it's never been an issue in your two-year relationship. One evening while talking about having children, your fiancé says he insists they be raised in his faith. *Deal breaker?*

*Y*ou're dating a guy who is a banker. He's clean-cut and in great shape. He invites you up to his apartment and the place is a pigsty: crusty dishes piled up in the sink and pubic hairs taking cover in every bathroom corner. *Deal breaker?*

*Y*ou finally get to see your new guy's apartment and are pleasantly surprised to see it's neater than yours! Upon further inspection you notice all the spice bottles and soup cans in the kitchen cabinets are perfectly aligned with the labels facing forward, and all of his CDs are alphabetized. When you make a comment about it, his reply is, "Everything has its place and there's no place for messiness." *Deal breaker?*

*Y*our new guy asks you back to his apartment, where he lives alone. When entering the bathroom, you notice a basket of rolled-up towels, potpourri, and fancy hand soap. *Deal breaker?*

You're engaged to a man who's of another religion and, when discussing wedding plans, he insists you follow the traditions of his faith during the ceremony. *Deal breaker?*

After three solid dates, he invites you over to his place for some Chinese food and a movie. While heating up the egg rolls he suggests you peruse his DVDs. You notice the entire collection consists of "chick flicks" such as *Runaway Bride, Sleepless in Seattle*, and *Boys on the Side*. *Deal breaker?*

You've been dating a cute guitarist for a couple of weeks and stumble upon a prescription for lithium in his apartment. *Deal breaker?*

You and your fiancé are having some guests over to your fabulous new apartment. When one of the guests praises it and says your fiancé made the right move by selling his vacation house in Florida, you're shocked and confused because he told you nothing about the sale. *Deal breaker?*

Your boyfriend wants to celebrate and invites you over for a romantic evening. When you ask to know the special occasion, he says he wants to christen the "nearly new" mattress he purchased at Sunday's neighborhood garage sale. *Deal breaker?*

Your boyfriend of one year was brought up in a religious household but hasn't been practicing as an adult. Earlier in the year he was in a car accident, which led him to rediscover his faith. Now he attends services at least three times a week and tries to persuade you to join him. *Deal breaker?*

You excuse yourself from the fabulous dinner your new guy has cooked to go to the bathroom. While looking for a new roll of toilet paper, you discover a box of tampons under the sink. When you ask jokingly if he has his period this week, he chuckles and goes on to explain he likes to have them handy "just in case." *Deal breaker?*

Your new guy invites you over to his place for what you hope turns into fun and games. Just as he pulls you down on his bed, you notice that hanging above the headboard is a picture of him lifting weights. *Deal breaker?*

After two months of dating you've been invited to stay at your boyfriend's country house for the weekend. When you tell him you've always been afraid of big old houses, he tells you not to worry because he keeps a gun in the main closet "for safety." *Deal breaker?*

*Y*ou're dating a guy who spends all vacations dedicated to community service projects organized by his church. *Deal breaker?*

*Y*our new guy invites you over to his place for dinner. He shows you around but steers you clear of one room, which he claims is for storage. While he's in the bathroom your curiosity gets the better of you, and you open the door to find the room filled with *Star Trek* convention paraphernalia and notebooks chronicling UFO sightings. *Deal breaker?*

*Y*ou and your guy have been dating for about six months and have gotten into the habit of staying at your place, since it's closer to where you both work. You begin to notice he never offers to do the dishes or take out the garbage. When you suggest little things he could do to contribute, he says, "But this is your place, not mine." *Deal breaker?*

*Y*ou've been seriously dating a man who's been married before. He had a child with his previous wife and then had a vasectomy. You know you want kids of your own one day, but he says he probably won't reverse the operation. *Deal breaker?*

*Y*ou're dating a guy who has an obsession with chewing gum. Over some time you notice he not only has packs of gum in nearly every nook and cranny of the house, but he sticks chewed pieces in various places—such as under tables and on coasters—"for later." *Deal breaker?*

*Y*our new guy suggests you go over to his place for a home-cooked meal that he is going to prepare. It's all *très* yummy until you end up spending the entire night praying to the porcelain god. *Deal breaker?*

You're waiting for your date to finish getting ready at his place when you notice some papers on his table. Upon "accidental inspection" you discover they're mood charts from his psychiatrist, indicating when to take his medication and instructing him to describe his feelings every day. *Deal breaker?*

Designated Drinker

Vices

You're getting serious with a guy who doesn't drink. When you probe the subject, he lets you know he spent some time in rehab but assures you he's completely sober now. *Deal breaker?*

♛

You're getting very serious with a man who's an accountant, and all signs point to him being "the one." One day he lets you know he's $30,000 in debt due to a sure thing known as *Funny Cide*, but he swears he's done with the ponies. *Deal breaker?*

You've been living with your guy for two years. One night he begins experiencing all the symptoms of a heart attack and you rush him to the hospital. After a couple of hours the doctor emerges from the ER to ask if you know he's been abusing drugs for the past year. *Deal breaker?*

You're getting very serious with a successful banker. Upon getting his Christmas bonus (which is a significant percent of his salary), he tells you he plans to take the next flight out to Vegas for his annual post-bonus gambling ritual. *Deal breaker?*

♛

You've been dating a guy and are really digging him. One day you run into each other on the street and unexpectedly see he's puffing away on a cigarette. When you confront him because you were positive he was a nonsmoker, he admits to smoking on occasion but just doesn't do it in front of you. *Deal breaker?*

You've been dating a man and decide to take your first vacation together. You're walking on the beach when he fishes out a dime bag of pot from his pocket. You ask where he got it and he says he brought it from home by hiding it in his shoe. *Deal breaker?*

*Y*ou and your boyfriend have been dating for three years. One day you log on to his computer to surf the Web and you see that nearly all the Web sites in his "Favorites" folder are porn. *Deal breaker?*

*Y*ou go with your boyfriend to your cousin's wedding, during which you notice he's been gone from the reception for quite a while, as has a member of the bridal party. You hear voices coming from the balcony and discover the two of them smoking pot together. *Deal breaker?*

*Y*ou and your new boyfriend have been invited to an engagement party at your friend's parents' house in the suburbs. He agrees to be the designated driver so that you can enjoy a glass of wine or two. At the end of the night you realize your guy is drunk and therefore you're forced to stay overnight. *Deal breaker?*

You've been dating a guy for a couple of months and decide to take a weekend trip together. You notice he has an alcoholic beverage with every meal: Bloody Mary at brunch, beer with lunch, and wine at dinner. When you ask him about it, he says, "I'm on vacation and that's how I relax." *Deal breaker?*

You initiate a conversation with your new guy about where things are headed. You've said your piece, and when it's time for him to express his feelings, he proceeds to slam back a few before he can talk openly. *Deal breaker?*

After four months of dating, you decide that your nephew's christening is the perfect place to introduce your boyfriend to the family. At the house reception he gets visibly drunk. *Deal breaker?*

You and your guy are driving to the theater when he stops at a mini-mart for gas. After paying and heading out the door, you see him hand a six-pack to a teenager who says, "Thanks a lot, mister." He gets in the car and says, "I know one guy who's going to have a good night tonight." *Deal breaker?*

♛

You stop at a mini-mart with the guy you're dating and he buys two hundred dollars' worth of lottery tickets. When you ask if he makes a habit of buying lottery tickets in bulk, he says, "If regularly means monthly, then yes." *Deal breaker?*

You're at a bar with a group of friends and the guy you're newly dating, who's a high school teacher, orders a pitcher of beer and says he wants to chug the whole thing just for you. *Deal breaker?*

He Coulda Been a Contender

Sports and Hobbies

*Y*our new beau invites you to a football game. When he picks you up, you can't help but notice his face is painted in team colors. He proceeds to cheer maniacally throughout the entire four quarters and every time you make a comment, he shushes you so he can focus. *Deal breaker?*

*Y*ou're planning your wedding, and the only day the reception site is available is Super Bowl Sunday. Your fiancé wants to postpone but the next available date is six months down the road. You don't want to wait but he's adamant about moving the wedding. *Deal breaker?*

*Y*ou've been asked out on a third date and can't wait. He surprises you with tickets to a baseball game. As you're driving to the stadium, you notice a package of Depend® undergarments in the car. When you ask what they're for, he lets you know he doesn't want to have to tear himself away from the game. And a beerless game is *not* an option. *Deal breaker?*

You've been waiting forty-five minutes at a restaurant for your date to show. Just as you finish your second glass of wine, he shows up and apologizes for running late, explaining he really needed to squeeze in a short workout. *Deal breaker?*

You're getting ready for your first date with a guy, but he cancels at the last minute because his best friend got tickets to a Knicks game. *Deal breaker?*

You and your new romantic interest head out for a friendly tennis match. He's delighted to win the first set, claiming his "swift serve" gives him the edge. When you win the second, he throws his racket on the court and demands a tiebreaker. You go on to win the third set and he says, "Whatever, I wasn't really trying that time anyway." *Deal breaker?*

*Y*ou and your new guy are watching ESPN. When the female sports commentator comes on to do the postgame interviews, he changes the channel and says, "There's nothing a woman's going to say about football that I need to hear." *Deal breaker?*

*Y*ou're surprised when you find out you and your new guy both work out at the same gym. One day he calls to ask if you'd like to join him at his favorite "All That Jazz" dancercise class. *Deal breaker?*

*Y*ou're doing the long-distance thing with a new guy and when you call to tell him your flight arrival time, he lets you know his sister will pick you up because you're arriving smack in the middle of the Yankees game. *Deal breaker?*

You get engaged on a Sunday, and Monday you take off for a business trip. One week after your return you discover your fiancé has bought a motorbike. When you question him about his secrecy, he says, "I thought you were going to be my wife, not my mother."
Deal breaker?

Your date asks you about your hobbies and when you say yoga and meditation, he responds, "I wouldn't have pegged you as someone to go for all that new agey, hippie stuff." *Deal breaker?*

Things are going really well between you and your boyfriend until one weekend he goes to see an astrologer who tells him that you are not his lifetime partner. You laugh it off but then he starts obsessing about it and can't get it out of his mind. *Deal breaker?*

*Y*ou're at your new beau's apartment and while waiting for him to get ready, you log on to his computer to use the Internet. You see he's recently purchased two swords and a jester's costume on medieval.com (and it's not for Halloween). *Deal breaker?*

*T*he man you've been seeing invites you up to his place. Upon entering, you notice that the book he's currently reading (which also has several pages that are dog-eared) is the hardcover version of Bob the Bachelor's *What a Difference a Year Makes*. *Deal breaker?*

*Y*ou're on a date with a guy, making great conversation. When you ask him who he'd like to lunch with out of anyone in the entire world (dead or alive), without hesitation he says, "Justin Timberlake." *Deal breaker?*

*Y*our boyfriend of one year is invited to compete on the TV show *Survivor*, which you encouraged him to do because you thought he'd have a great chance of winning. Unfortunately, he doesn't win, and when the series airs, he comes off looking like a total jerk. He claims it's due to editing, but now everyone has this horrible impression of him. It's even hard to go out in public without someone making a rude comment. *Deal breaker?*

✺

*Y*ou get to talking with the cute guy sitting next to you at the bar and when you ask if he has any hobbies, he says hunting because there's "nothing like the first kill of the season." *Deal breaker?*

☂

*Y*ou ask about your new guy's celebrity crushes and he let's you know he's always had a thing for Pamela Anderson. You shrug it off until you see that he TiVo's *Baywatch* every night and has several magazines with the actress adorning the cover. *Deal breaker?*

*Y*our beau of one month invites you over for dinner and while he's cooking, you click on to *The West Wing*. When you ask him what's up with the smirk on his face, he explains he only watches the news because everything else is inane and mindless. *Deal breaker?*

*Y*ou're getting into a very animated and heated discussion with your date about World War II. As a history buff you love every minute of it. Just as the waiter is bringing over his apple strudel, he tells you he strongly believes Hitler was the greatest leader known to mankind. *Deal breaker?*

*Y*ou're on a date, telling the guy about the fabulous novel you're reading. He says he's so impressed because he's never actually read a book cover to cover. *Deal breaker?*

You're perusing your new guy's CD collection and notice he doesn't have any rock albums. When you ask him about it, he says he refuses to listen to anything but classical and jazz because "that's *real* music" that has stood the test of time. *Deal breaker?*

Honking the Car Horn

Manners

*Y*ou've locked in a second date with the guy you met last week, and can't wait. He lets you know he'll pick you up at eight. While you're getting ready you hear him honking his car horn, waiting for you to come out. *Deal breaker?*

👍

*Y*ou can't help but notice on the past couple of dates that your guy gets overly friendly with the waitresses, chatting with them and always finding out their names. When you ask him about it, he claims he's just being friendly. *Deal breaker?*

👎

*Y*our parents have finally taken the big step to invite you and your new beau to dinner. Things are going great until you nearly choke on a crab cake when you overhear your guy telling Mom and Dad a dirty joke that involves excessive cursing and references to body parts you'd really rather not discuss with your parents. *Deal breaker?*

*Y*our date reserved a table at the new, hip downtown sushi place. At the end of the meal you notice he never removed his baseball cap. *Deal breaker?*

👍

*Y*our new guy is in great shape and quite health-conscious. He's got a strict exercise routine and his fridge is filled with organic products. One night you're out to dinner, and when you order a burger and fries, he says, "Are you sure you want to eat that? That's at least two days' worth of fat grams." *Deal breaker?*

👎

*Y*ou're at a bar with a guy having some drinks and enjoying the conversation. When you sit down to dinner you notice his stories aren't nearly as riveting when told with an open mouth full of steak and mashed potatoes. *Deal breaker?*

*Y*ou and your date are enjoying a nice dinner. When the waiter approaches to ask if you'd like some more wine, you say "Yes, thank you" but your date interrupts with "No, I think we've both had quite enough." *Deal breaker?*

👎

*Y*ou and your date are walking through the park when he opens up a chocolate bar and throws the wrapper on the ground. When you make a comment about his littering, he assures you one wrapper isn't going to make a difference. *Deal breaker?*

👍

*Y*our guy has a really bad relationship with dairy products and is totally in denial about his lactose intolerance. He continues to eat foods such as cheese and ice cream when you're together, fully aware you're going to suffer through the aftereffects. *Deal breaker?*

*Y*ou're out on a second date having drinks with a guy and neither of you can deny there's a spark. You make a comment about how you liked him from the get-go. He smiles and tells you he likes you too and adds he's always liked bigger women. *Deal breaker?*

👎

*Y*ou're going on a double date with your guy's best friend and his new girlfriend, Julie. On the way home, your boyfriend says, "Julie is really hot. You should get your hair cut like her." *Deal breaker?*

👍

*Y*ou've noticed that while your new guy always opens the door for you and lets you in the elevator first, he hardly ever extends the same courtesy to other women. *Deal breaker?*

👎

*Y*ou and your beau have lively discussions. On the rare occasion when you don't agree, he shushes you in the middle of arguing and refuses to listen to what you have to say. *Deal breaker?*

*Y*ou've begun dating a guy whose motto is "Happy people aren't concerned with time," so he doesn't wear a watch and tends to stay away from devices that "track him down." While you're loving the fact that he's so laid-back, you've noticed it's challenging to make plans because even though he has an answering machine, he rarely checks it, and gets back to you days after you call. *Deal breaker?*

👍

*Y*our girlfriend invites you and your new beau over to her house for a barbecue. A few hours (and beers) later, you see him meander over to a nearby bush. When you let him know the bathroom is only fifty feet away, he shrugs it off, claiming he's "helping out with the drought." *Deal breaker?*

*Y*ou've been on a business trip for two long weeks, and you and your new boyfriend can't wait to see each other. You call to ask if he'll pick you up from the airport as you don't want another moment to go by without seeing him. But he refuses, explaining he doesn't want to do something he's never going to continue to do in the future. *Deal breaker?*

👍

*Y*ou're fifteen minutes late for a date because a meeting ran over. You apologize profusely and explain you would've called if you'd had his cell phone number. He goes on to tell you he refuses to get a cell because he believes they're an "excuse for bad behavior, and people should be where they say they're going to be."
Deal breaker?

*Y*ou and your new guy head out to your parents' golf club for a swim on the first day of summer. You lather up with sunscreen while your guy heads straight to the diving board. Just as you bury your head in a book, you hear him yell, "Honey! Look at me!" and he proceeds to do one cannonball after another. *Deal breaker?*

👎

*Y*our job takes you to a foreign country where the time difference is sixteen hours. The guy you've been dating for a month accidentally calls you in the middle of the night and apologizes for miscalculating the time. He then continues to call at that same time throughout your trip, explaining it's the only time that works for him. *Deal breaker?*

"It's Not You, It's . . . You"

Character

*Y*ou're meeting a guy for drinks at the local pub during the always-crowded happy hour. A woman accidentally bumps into your date, and as she walks by he yells, "Watch it, you fat bitch!" *Deal breaker?*

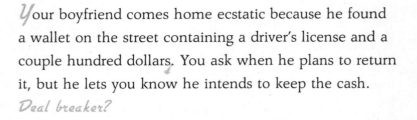

*Y*ou've been casually dating a guy who is trying his hand at stand-up comedy and he invites you to his first show. You're shocked to find all the material centers around the personal details of your relationship. *Deal breaker?*

*Y*our boyfriend comes home ecstatic because he found a wallet on the street containing a driver's license and a couple hundred dollars. You ask when he plans to return it, but he lets you know he intends to keep the cash. *Deal breaker?*

*Y*ou're dating a guy who asks to borrow some socks since his got wet while walking in the rain. Two weeks later you ask for them back and he says, "Can't you just buy a new pair? I'm pretty confident you can spare the two-fifty." *Deal breaker?*

♥

*Y*ou've been on several dates with a guy and notice he's never told one joke the whole time you've been together. In fact, he's never even laughed at one of yours. *Deal breaker?*

♥

*Y*ou and your new guy decide to take your niece to the petting zoo. You can't wait to see how he will interact with her. Although he's getting along great with your niece, he's taunting all the animals. *Deal breaker?*

♥

*Y*ou've been asked out by the cute guy you met the other night. He tells you he's thirty, but when you catch a glimpse of his driver's license, it indicates he's thirty-six. *Deal breaker?*

*Y*ou've been laid up in bed for three days with a horrible flu. Your boyfriend stops by on the premise that he's bringing you chicken soup and a bottle of ginger ale. Before you even take your first sip, he's undoing your robe and trying to get inside your pajama pants. *Deal breaker?*

♥

*Y*our boyfriend of six months gives you a necklace with a religious icon for your birthday. When you remind him of your agnostic beliefs he says, "But you believe in some kind of a higher power, and it's really just a symbol." *Deal breaker?*

💔

*Y*our new boyfriend tells you he graduated from Brown University. He invites you to meet his parents over Thanksgiving. During dinner they ask if he's planning on going to his five-year college reunion. You jump in saying you've always wanted to visit Rhode Island. His parents respond, "Rhode Island? But Kingsborough Community College is in *Brooklyn*." *Deal breaker?*

*Y*our boyfriend proposes to you and presents you with a beautiful ring in a Tiffany's box! You're ecstatic, and the next day you take it to get appraised for insurance purposes. After the examination the jeweler tells you it's a cubic zirconium, and apparently your boyfriend knew it. *Deal breaker?*

♥

*Y*ou and your man are taking a stroll along the beach when you overhear a toddler crying for his mommy. Your boyfriend turns in the kid's direction and utters, "Oh shut up, you whiney brat." *Deal breaker?*

♥

*Y*ou and your boyfriend are out shopping and get into a fender bender in the mall parking lot. Some arguing ensues and, even though it's not clear who's at fault, your boyfriend makes a comment under his breath about how women shouldn't be allowed behind the wheel. *Deal breaker?*

*Y*ou're dating a gorgeous Colombian artist who came to the States to study painting. When you suggest taking a vacation together, he tells you he can't leave the country because he's here on a student visa, which expired two years ago. *Deal breaker?*

♥

*Y*ou're dating a real gentleman who opens doors, carries bags, and regularly brings you flowers. After a couple of months you suggest he cook dinner, but he retorts, "Me, cook? If it's not in the garage, it's not my job."
Deal breaker?

💔

*Y*ou and your boyfriend have a deal: whenever you cook dinner, he brings dessert. No matter how many times you remind him you're allergic to nuts, he continues to bring over desserts such as maple walnut ice cream and pecan pie. *Deal breaker?*

You've been making eyes at the cute guy with the chocolate lab in the dog park every Saturday and he finally asks you out. On your third date he admits to "borrowing" his friend's dog once a week because he knew it would be the ultimate chick magnet.
Deal breaker?

♥

At first you were delighted with the fact that your new beau is so agreeable, but six months have passed and even now, whenever you ask him what he wants to do, his response is always, "I don't care, babe, what do *you* want to do?" *Deal breaker?*

💔

You're out to dinner with two other couples and having a great conversation. When one of the women mentions Oprah and how many people her Angel Network has helped, your guy jumps in and says, "But more importantly, is she skinny or fat this year?"
Deal breaker?

You're engaged to the man of your dreams. One night after many drinks he admits that the play he wrote (which was also just recently produced on Broadway) was actually someone else's idea; he stole it. *Deal breaker?*

You're out on a third date with a guy who suggests going to dinner and a movie. When you arrive at the theater you discover the movie you both wanted to see is sold out. He proceeds to throw a fit, cursing the fact that he didn't buy tickets over the phone and saying the "whole night is ruined." *Deal breaker?*

The guy you've been out on a couple of dates with picks you up at eight. On the way to the restaurant another driver cuts him off and he starts hitting the steering wheel and cursing at the driver. The next thing you know, he's driving like a madman, weaving in and out of traffic and chasing the other driver. *Deal breaker?*

You've been engaged for a year and the wedding day is quickly approaching. Your fiancé works in the entertainment business and comes home with the news that you can be on a reality TV show called *Should They Say "I Do!"?* and make a nice sum of money. Apparently, without you knowing, he's placed cameras in the kitchen since you've been engaged, and the episodes have already been edited. The tape just needs to be submitted with your approval. *Deal breaker?*

♥

The guy you're dating calls in a huff because he just got recruited for jury duty, which he feels is not worth his time. The next day he calls to tell you he got out of sitting on an armed robbery case because he made up a story in which *he'd* been robbed years earlier. *Deal breaker?*

♥

You and your boyfriend of four months are having your first fight. Just when you think things are cooling down, he asks if you're "on the rag." *Deal breaker?*

*W*hile stopping at the pharmacy, you see your new guy parked in a handicapped spot. When you comment on it, he says he won't be more than fifteen minutes and tells you no one ever parks in those spots anyway. *Deal breaker?*

British Words Are Cooler

Hodgepodge

*Y*ou meet a cute guy in a bar who seems really interesting and quite witty. You exchange e-mail addresses and he promises to write the next day. When reading his e-mail you notice it's laden with grammatical errors. *Deal breaker?*

*Y*ou invite your new guy over to your house for a barbecue. He shows up with a bowl of potato salad and his dog, Rusty. Just as you've finished preparing the juicy steaks you bought, he throws one more on the grill just for Rusty. *Deal breaker?*

*T*he guy you've been flirting with at a party asks you out. Throughout the conversation you notice he uses British words such as "flat," "bin," and "loo," but has no accent. When you ask about his choice of vocabulary, he explains he once vacationed in London and thinks certain British words are cooler. *Deal breaker?*

*Y*our date asks what type of food you want for dinner, and when you suggest French, he refuses because of France's stance on the war in Iraq. *Deal breaker?*

*Y*ou're on your third date with a guy and talking about your families and backgrounds. When you proudly show off a picture of your adorable niece, he reciprocates with a picture of his dog that he carries in his wallet. *Deal breaker?*

*Y*ou and your new love interest are enjoying your second date together by taking a long walk through the park. When you pass a group of children hanging on the monkey bars, he lets you know how many kids he wants and the names he's picked out for them. *Deal breaker?*

*Y*ou and your new beau have been invited to a friend's housewarming party in the suburbs. When you get lost on the way, he refuses to ask for directions. Forty-five minutes later he's still looking at the map, trying to figure out what went wrong. *Deal breaker?*

*Y*ou're dating a guy who's so in love with his golden retriever he will only go on vacations to places where his dog can join you. *Deal breaker?*

*Y*ou've been on a couple of dates with a guy who, no matter what you do or say, continues to flatter you with phrases such as "You're the smartest girl I've ever met," "Your life is so perfect," and "I'm not sure I deserve you." *Deal breaker?*

*Y*ou're so excited that your girls' vacation to St. Thomas is finally here. While you're away, the guy you've been dating for a month calls you every day to tell you how much he misses you and says, "How can you possibly feel good about going there without me?" *Deal breaker?*

*Y*ou meet a really cute guy in a bar and make plans to go on a date. You give him your e-mail address and when he contacts you, you see his e-mail name is "Wildinthesack." *Deal breaker?*

*E*lection Day is just around the corner and when you ask your new guy who he's going to vote for, he says no one because he isn't registered. *Deal breaker?*

*Y*ou love the fact that the guy you've been dating for the last few weeks has a respectable job as a business consultant and is very well-mannered. One evening he gets a phone call from his friend and you notice he's suddenly using phrases such as "Right on, dude," "Hang loose, bro," and "Excellent, my main man"—language which is inconsistent with all the conversations you've had together. *Deal breaker?*

*A*fter six months of dating, you suggest taking a trip with your new beau and he agrees. When you recommend Italy, he lets you know he won't go anywhere that requires getting on an airplane because he's afraid to fly. *Deal breaker?*

*Y*ou arrange to meet your new guy at the park to play Frisbee. You see him pull up on his motorcycle and notice his pet dog is strapped into the passenger seat, sporting a mini helmet. *Deal breaker?*

You are getting very serious with a man who says that when he decides to marry, he will insist on eloping because he doesn't want to deal with the hassle that goes along with a big wedding. *Deal breaker?*

❧

You're out with your guy and his friends playing "Truth or Dare." One of the friends asks, "What's the craziest thing you've ever done?" and he admits arranging to have his car stolen several years ago so he could claim the insurance to buy a better car. *Deal breaker?*

❧

Your new beau's best friend is a stunning woman. *Deal breaker?*

❧

You and your boyfriend have been going out for about six months when he gives you a gorgeous bracelet. Later you find out he gives that exact same bracelet to every woman after six months of dating. *Deal breaker?*

*Y*ou've gone out on a couple of dates with a guy who lets you know he's been arrested more than once for getting into fights in bars. *Deal breaker?*

*T*he guy you're seeing, who is from a very affluent family, invites you to a fancy work function. On the way there he requests that you not mention where you're from, if anyone asks. *Deal breaker?*

Acknowledgments

Without Carlos Caicedo, Elizabeth Dunkel, and David Ruth, this book truly might never have been. We are so thankful to them for giving us just a tiny bit of their enormous talents.

We'd like to thank our agent, Agnes Birnbaum, who showed great enthusiasm for the book from day one, and our editor, Rebecca Cole, who saw our vision and truly made the book come to life.

We are grateful to Barbara Eliason for all her legal work and for always having our best interests at heart.

Writing this book wouldn't have been nearly as fun without our clients and friends from Kimberly-Clark:

Trisha Witt-DeVine, Nathan Hanson, Kurt Simon, and Jermel Carr. They were there from the beginning.

Thank you to Laurel Richie for being such an important mentor to both of us.

We'd like to thank Rose Abdoo for her invaluable creative input, Rosalie Siegel and Kevin Kelly for their very helpful suggestions, Carol Dronsfield for making us look good on a hot day, and all our friends for their personal "Deal Breaker" stories.

Thank you to our families for their support. And to John Engel for being worth the wait.

About the Authors

MICHELE AVANTARIO was born in Brooklyn, New York, and began her career as a television and radio advertising producer in Manhattan. She currently runs her own casting and wrangling company, working with babies and toddlers in the United States and internationally. Michele lives in New York with her new husband, John.

New York native MAIA DUNKEL is a successful advertising executive in Manhattan. She has a master's degree in Russian language and culture, and lived in Russia for four years. Currently living and dating in New York City, Maia is the occasional stand-up comedian.